LIVING
Beyond
AWESOME

*The inspiring story of one ordinary mom's
quest to use her God-given abilities to
push her body, mind, and spirit
beyond the limit*

by
Jen McDonough

PUBLISHED BY 3D PUBLISHING

Library of Congress Control Number: 2011941820

ISBN 13: 978-0984770403
ISBN: 0984770402
3D Publishing
Lindstrom, MN

"**Living Beyond Awesome** *is a refreshing glimpse into the demands, struggles and joys a family shares together when one of its members decides to train for 'The Ironman'.*

As a sports retail store owner for over 27 years, I have seen many Ironman persons and have participated in six Ironmans myself. At times I have taken what I and others do for granted. Often I have minimized and hid from my family and friends the training I do and the stress that it causes me in my job and relationships. Jen's emotional account of her family involvement and support of her husband and children illustrate how pursuing a major goal, be it an Ironman, or any other significant undertaking, can create additional richness and strength within the family. Jen's story shows how family members all shared in her victory of the Ironman because everyone shared in the making of it. It's an example that many of us can embrace when someone in their family chooses to push the envelope."

   —**JAN GUENTHER**, *6-Time Ironman Finisher, Owner of Gear West Ski & Run, Competitive Cross Country Skier, and Madison Ironman Record Course Holder*

"*Warning: the events depicted in this book may inspire you to accomplish "unreachable" goals. Although triathlon is about swimming, cycling and running,* **Living Beyond Awesome** *is about much more. Jen McDonough's journey to become and Iron-mom is a triumph of the human spirit, and reminds us all that we can do much more than we ever thought possible . . . if only we "Don't quet!"*

   —**KEVIN BURNS**, *Exercise physiology PhD, 5-time Ironman finisher, & 2-time Kona qualifier.*

"**Living Beyond Awesome** *will make you laugh and make you cry. You will be inspired to do anything you set your mind to do after reading this inspiring story. If Jen McDonough can do it, so can you!*"

—**BRIDGET SIEBENALER,** *Ironman Finisher*

"**Living Beyond Awesome,** *by Jen McDonough is an inspiration to all people. Athletes, moms, pastors and others would truly benefit themselves by reading this book. The way Jen fights the external conflicts of a family in need of her, the fatigue of her training, and the exhaustion of the race to become an Ironman would make anyone who strives to reach a goal smile. The way she depicts what is going on inside of her head gives the book a sense of character that can make you feel like you are actually in her shoes, or right there beside her as she battles the elements of the Ironman. Overall, this piece of literature is a well written, quality story of a conflict and a goal that is achieved by hard work and perseverance, with a little help from God. I believe this book will be a hit. You go Jen! Never Quet!*"

—**JACKIE WALTERS,** *Personal Finance Coach & Mom.*

*Dedicated to
my mom . . . the strongest person I know.*

"Don't Quet!"

—MAGGIE MCDONOUGH

❋

*To my family, friends, and to those
who bless me by reading our story:*

*When life tries to knock you down, keep
moving forward. Just keep on
swimming, don't quet.*

*It's okay if your goals need change, just
keep moving forward, don't quet.*

*Most of all, keep having faith in
God, don't quet!*

—JEN MCDONOUGH

Contents

Discipline in our private
lives shows up in our
public lives.

—BOB MERRITT,
Senior Pastor, Eagle Brook Church

CHAPTER 1

I Am *Not* a Swimmer!

I am not a swimmer.

I stood on the beach, my bare feet scrunching the cool, fine sand between my toes. It was 6:40 A.M., the first Saturday in November, and I was about to embark on the biggest sporting adventure of my life!

There was a chill in the air. I shivered, facing the massive body of water before me. The first signs of daylight filtered through the dark skies as it cast glowing rays on the ocean Sounds, time and sights seemed surreal. Was I really here? Had this day finally come? What the heck am I doing? Where's my life jacket? Arm floaties? Can I just go home?

Whatever my fears, at least I knew I was not alone. There were over 2,000 of us standing together on Panama Beach that cool crisp morning—every one preparing to embark on this same adventure, the Florida Ironman Triathlon. Most of us were dressed similarly, in thick full-body suits and swim caps in the hope that these form-fitting garments would help preserve some of our body warmth in the cold elements. We looked like tall penguins, all crunched in together, nervously milling around.

The sense of excitement, anxiety, and apprehension in the air pushed my senses into high alert, I could hear myself taking deep breaths, trying to calm my anxious nerves.

I was about to partake, willingly, in what I knew might be one of the scariest moments in my life —a 2.4 mile swim in the Gulf of Mexico. The rolling waves looked massive to me, and I tried not to puke. I just knew I'd end up being eaten by a shark! In fact, when we'd fished these same waters the day before, the boat captain had bragged about the 12 foot hammerhead shark they'd recently caught off these shores. I think my husband saw me turn pale at the mention of this, as he quickly changed the "shark" conversation back to the weather.

As I looked around, I thought of how lucky I was to be here this brisk November morning. Some 2000+ entry slots had opened up one year ago for this event. Those of us standing on the beach today were fortunate to have snagged a coveted slot.

Getting in to an Ironman Triathlon event is a big deal. There are less than two dozen of these events held at various locations around the world each year. The Florida Ironman usually fills up just minutes after online registration opens—one whole year before the actual event. I remembered how excited I'd been when I'd registered last year. Now, I wondered, "what was I thinking?"

Several weeks before registration had opened up, I'd asked my husband to consider choosing one of two things I very much wanted: A fourth baby, or an Ironman. It was a long week in waiting for the answer. Did he hear me? Should I bring it up again? Did he forget?

A week later, Bob asked what Ironman event I was going to do. I was beyond elated! Not only had he heard me, but he was giving me the thumbs up to pursue a dream.

An Ironman Triathlon consists of a 2.4 mile swim, followed by a 112 mile bike ride, and a 26.2 mile run (a full marathon). The event begins at 7:00 A.M., and ends at midnight. In order to finish, you must complete all three events by midnight. Finish before midnight, and you earn the title of "Ironman." If you finish after the midnight deadline, you are disqualified. Each of the three events has an individual time limit, as well.

With ordinary talent and extraordinary perseverance, all things are attainable.

—Thomas Foxwell Buxton

CHAPTER 2

I Am *Not* an Athlete!

Training for an Ironman is a sacrifice that many do not understand. Even I didn't understand fully, before I started. B.C. (before children), I had competed in Olympic-style weightlifting events for over 10 years. When I say this, most people picture an extremely muscular person who poses, or a person who is doing a bench press. Olympic-style weightlifting is neither of these. Simply put, Olympic-style lifting is an anaerobic sport (no aerobic type activity involved) meaning that it is basically the opposite sport of triathlon. The two sports are on total opposite ends of the spectrum when it comes to similarities on how you train for them and what your body is trained to do. Olympic weightlifting requires every muscle fiber in one's body to lift as much weight overhead as humanly possible. Each lift is literally completed in seconds. It requires strength, years of refining one's technique, and, as with any dedicated sport, a great amount of confidence and belief in one's self.

My weight training started off with lifting a broomstick when I was 17 years old. I was the youngest of four kids in my family and the only girl. My older brother Mike liked to lift weights when he was a teenager and could bench-press more than most of the kids in high school. I admired him a great deal and I wanted to be able to lift like him when I got older. When I started playing around in the gym in high school, I had no idea what I was doing. I was just a skinny kid who just enjoyed reading up and learning about lifting weights.

I competed against many Olympic-style weightlifters who were considered natural athletes. Things came easy for them. With me, I was *not* a natural athlete and worked hard to make it up in areas I could control such as discipline and perseverance. I knew that if I stuck to a plan, my nonathletic body would be stretched to its maximum potential.

Throughout my weightlifting journey, I was blessed to have qualified for and competed in eight national championships and I held countless state records in several weight categories. I was also honored and blessed to have competed in two United States Olympic Festivals.

While all of this sounds impressive, weightlifting is very different kind of activity than the Ironman would require.

Weightlifting is usually completed in a quick burst of lifting motions, lasting only seconds, followed by a rest. Lift and rest, lift and rest. So we're talking very brief "spurts" of exertion, whereas aerobic exercise involves longer periods of constant activity. My previous experience with aerobic didn't leave the fondest of memories. . .

During my weightlifting training, I tried to ride the stationary bike with one of my teammates. After 10 minutes, I was dying (well, that's how it felt, anyway). It took me weeks to get up to 24 minutes a workout, and then I was still exhausted. So, even with years of training and competing in a brutal Olympic style lifting sport, Ironman was very intimidating to me. I never thought my anaerobic muscle fibers could make it through a totally aerobic endurance event like Ironman.

Here I was today trying to compete in an Ironman which was a far cry from my former life. Could it be done? I sure hoped so.

Shoot for the moon.
Even if you miss,
you'll land
among the stars.

—Les Brown

CHAPTER 3

Sign Me Up!

The first goal was to gain entry into the Ironman event after I had gotten the okay from Bob.

Registration for Ironman Florida was just a few weeks away and I decided that this body would probably do best on the flat biking and running course that Florida offered. I decided to go for it and knew that gaining entry would require preparation in itself. Each day I would wonder if I would gain entry for the event.

On the morning registration opened up, I woke up with a sense of nervous energy. Would I be able to get through to register? I had heard many stories of people who had tried for several years to gain an entry, but who were unsuccessful.

I was grateful to my kind neighbor Laura who let me use her computer to get registered. My hands were poised and ready to start typing minutes before registration opened up. Credit card and USA Triathlon membership card were ready to go. Tick, tick, tick. Two minutes before the screen read that registration was officially open, I started clicking on the entry link. On the third try, the page opened! I was elated, but also knew I had to type as fast as possible. My entry would not be complete until I hit the submit button. Good grief, there seemed to be a lot of questions! I typed, fast and furious. My occupation as an executive administrative assistant paid off here. My fingers flew across the keyboard. No breathing until the "submit entry" button was hit. . .

I thought of a person I'd run into recently, who said he'd tried for three years to get into this event. One time, just when he'd made it to the point of hitting the "submit entry" button, the system kicked him out, followed by a "Sorry, this event is full" message! How heartbreaking! I tried not to think of this, as I hit the button. . .

I must have had God on my side, because when I hit "enter" it flashed back "ENTRY ACCEPTED"!

Really? Had I really gotten in? I was beyond excited! I stood in Laura's living room, blabbing away about how lucky and blessed I felt.

I couldn't wait to tell my family and friends. I knew my husband, Bob, would be excited for me but I had a slight fear of telling my friends. It was a huge commitment to make. Saying it out loud seemed to make it real. What if I failed? Everyone would know.

When I got home, Bob was so very sweet. He was excited, too, and shared the news with our three kids, who were all under the age of 8-years-old. The kids didn't quite understand it, but knew that whatever it was, it made me very happy.

I e-mailed Alan, from my biking crew, and Kevin, a friend from work, first. I knew they would both understand the excitement of getting into the event, having done this before. Alan had just completed his first Ironman two months earlier in Madison, Wisconsin, and Kevin is a top contender in his age group. After hitting the "send" button with my exciting news, I couldn't help but wonder, if they would read the e-mail and think, "What on earth is she doing? She's not Ironman material"? Their enthusiastic responses made me grin. "Well what the heck, just put that fear of failure behind you and tell the rest of the gang of friends," I thought. When I received droves of well wishes, encouragement, and support, I was so glad I had shared the news that I was going to become an Ironman!

Next came finding a training program that would work. Honestly, I am not really an athlete. I like to pretend I am, and have a blast pretending. Most people think of a sleek, muscular physique when you mention being an Ironman. I am not. I carry my 185 lbs around well, but at 5'7" tall, I can only hide so much of my mass. I am a mom to three kids (ages 7, 6, and 5), a wife, and I worked full time with a daily 2+ hour commute. I would need to find a program that could work around our lives (versus one that would take over our lives). My goal was to finish, and finish injury free, if possible. If I was a little slower, that was just fine.

There are **many** training programs available. It was a bit daunting to read through books, websites, and magazine articles looking for the right one. The program needed to "connect" with me—I didn't want a 100 page spreadsheet that required a master's degree to understand. It had to be clearly written and easy to understand. I knew that picking the top champion training programs would only set me up for failure. I needed an "average person" program — one that would not alienate me from my family or work when all was said and done.

After researching many programs, I found Don Fink's *Be Iron-Fit* program that seemed perfect with our busy lifestyle. It was a 30-week training program that had an average of 12 hours per week of training. Training was calculated by time, rather than by miles or laps. It was much lower in terms of training time than many programs out there, but hundreds of people who had busy lives had followed the program and had successfully completed their Ironman journey. It was perfect for what I needed.

I was a bit like Dustin Hoffman in Rainman as I had to have a book on me at all times! One in my bike bag, one in my swim bag, etc. I think I bought all of the copies our local books store had. I knew it was important for me to never feel lost on what I was doing each day.

I also enjoyed reading inspirational books about Ironman training tips as well as stories about people's experiences during their first Ironman. I would read those stories over and over again early on in my training. It helped to be inspired by those that had crossed the finish line ahead of me.

Next came the evaluation of my equipment. When I say this, many athletes can probably relate to what this process is like. Is what I have good enough to get me through this grueling event? When you start looking for an excuse to buy new equipment, it doesn't take much to go into the "I want/need" mode versus just being satisfied with what you have. If you want things, there are always people willing to sell them to you.

I ended up picking out my dream triathlon bike. The frame was made of lightweight carbon fiber. It was last year's model, and listed for around $3,600. We got it for a bargain price of ONLY $2,300 (more than we paid for any of our current vehicles), and put it on our nearly maxed-out credit card. I know what many non-bikers are saying at this point: How can something with a frame and some wheels cost so much? Incredibly, at $2,300, this was considered a lower-end carbon triathlon bike. I had once thought the same thing, when we bought my $800 road bike!

Every day (almost every waking hour!) for an **entire year**, I thought about what this moment on the beach would feel like, and questioned my ability to actually do this. I thought of my past. I was an accomplished weightlifter, I'd made it on a women's professional football team (that's a story for another book), and I was a mom three times over. Yet there I was, overwhelmed at the thought of the physical training required just to prepare to compete in an Ironman event.

On most days I had a positive attitude. However, there were some days my attitude waivered, and I thought, "What the heck am I doing? I am not an athlete. I'm just a regular person who loves to exercise." I needed to keep a positive attitude as much as possible. I knew negativity feeds on itself, and would only lead to my eventual failure. I struggled to keep negative thoughts away on days when I was either physically tired, had succumbed to poor eating habits, and/or was overtraining. I also fought negativity on days when I was feeling emotionally drained from the stresses of juggling work, family, training and other commitments.

Don't say you don't have enough time. You have exactly the same number of hours per day that were given to Helen Keller, Pasteur, Michaelangelo, Mother Teresa, Leonardo da Vinci, Thomas Jefferson, and Albert Einstein.

—Life's Little Instruction Book, *compiled by H. Jackson Brown, Jr.*

CHAPTER 4

Who Has Time?

The keys to my success would include learning great time management skills, staying intentionally focused on my goal, listening to my body, and sticking to my plan. Learning to listen to my body and following my plan when it called for rest did not come naturally for me. On days I would feel tired, my body would tell me to cut back, but my mind would shout, "You will fail, if you don't stick to the plan." Trying to ease up a bit at times when fatigue set in was very hard. My mind was conditioned to the idea that "more" was better. I had to learn that my training plan was my map to success, and sticking to it as much as possible would be my best chance for becoming an Ironman. Straying too far from it would likely mean not reaching my goal.

I learned to hone my time-management skills a great deal. Time was narrowed down to family, training and work. Bedtime was no later than 9:00 P.M. Most days, I was up by 3:30 or 4:00 A.M., so

I could train before work. Three of my mornings started out at the YMCA for an hour swim with a short bike or run thrown in before or after. Other mornings, I would run or bike from 1 to 1-1/2 hours. In the evening, I usually took a 30 minute to 3-hour bike, and/or run, but only doing so around our kids' schedules.

On weekends I let myself sleep in until 5:30 A.M. I tried to get my workouts in as early as possible so they wouldn't disrupt our family time. My goal was to be done by 11:00 A.M. Saturdays were usually saved up for my long bike rides (3–6 hours) with a ½ to 1-hour run afterwards. Sundays were saved for a quick 30 minute bike ride and a 2–4 hour run.

On shorter runs, I could be found running at the park with our kids. While they were playing in the sandbox, swinging on swings, and sliding down slides, I was running round and round the park —for literally miles at a time—to make my time goal. On other days, my kids could be found biking alongside me as I ran. Would it have been easier to 'train without the kids? Definitely, but I am telling you, the reward for having trained with and around my kids is a treasure I will always cherish. Each mile logged running at the park with my children is a lasting memory that can instantly turn my frown-face into a smile.

During the longer summer days, I rode my bike into work. I would leave our house at the break of dawn to bike 45 miles through country roads and then manipulate through downtown city traffic. One such morning, my bare legs and toes were very cold and mist was coming from my lips when I exhaled. What the heck? I reached for my water bottles. Darn, I forgot that I had frozen them the night before so they would stay icy cold on my ride. They hadn't melted like they should have—they were blocks of ice! On the way in, I read a bank sign that said it was 42° out! No wonder I couldn't feel my toes. I thought, "What has this got to do with being an Ironman? I'm freezing!" Was I building character? No, I was just doing my darnedest not to get frost bite!

My husband and kids especially liked when I biked or ran part-way home from work. Bob would stop the van, turn to me with a big grin, and say, "Get out!" It always made the kids and me laugh. I think maybe he'd always wanted to say this! It seemed so strange to be dropped off on a rural country road with no one around. By the time I would get home, he had supper going and the kids were working on homework.

I had become a master at time management by fitting in my workouts around our family versus having my family time worked in around my training.

If you aim at nothing, you will hit it every time.

—Zig Ziglar

CHAPTER 5

We All Need Goals!

Unlike the past few weeks of training in our somewhat cool climate, I was looking forward to perfect weather on the day of this event. Time was drawing nearer to the 7:00 A.M. gun start, and I was getting more anxious as the seconds ticked by. The swim portion was the first event, and it really scared me. I was "not a swimmer."

In preparation for this day, I'd taken lessons from a world-class swimmer who had crossed the English Channel. He was a certified coach and told me my stroke looked like I was "trying to swim without drowning." I knew that had to be fixed, or my chances of completing the 2.4 mile swim portion of the event would be low. I booked six swim lessons. I took our 8-year-old Maggie with me, as the cost was the same for two. I thought it would be a fun activity to learn together. While I struggled to make my limbs move the way we were taught,

Maggie was lapping the pool like she'd been doing this her entire life. She was an inspiration and it turned out to be a phenomenal mom and daughter venture.

This new swim stroke felt foreign. For the first few months, each and every stroke felt so unnatural. I would leave some swim workouts feeling frustrated and inept. It took a few months before it finally felt like I was actually "swimming." While I dreaded getting up in the morning to trudge my way to the pool, I always felt great after my crack of dawn workout swims. The hours spent listening to my underwater MP3 headphones while my body stretched out with each stroke was wonderful. I especially loved it towards the end of summer when I swam with the moon as my source of overhead light in the outdoor pool before it closed in the fall. For several months, the faint smell of chlorine clung to my skin throughout the day . . . I actually began to like the smell after awhile.

My biggest mental obstacle was that I had never swum over 1.2 miles before. Now my plan was to complete twice that distance (2.4 miles) on the day of the event. My plan said not to worry about never having done a full distance swim during training — I was very much counting on my plan working for me!

The sun was beginning to make its way up over the Gulf of Mexico, and we would soon be starting. I took time to mentally review the top three swim goals I had set for myself:

1. Finish the swim within the 2 hour and 20 minute time limit.
2. Try not to get eaten by a shark (my kids told me sharks liked "yum, yum yellow" so I was sure to NOT wear ANY yellow for the swim!)
3. Don't drown.

As my toes wiggled nervously through the sand, I looked out at the endless body of water. Wow! Those swells were pretty huge! Were those shark fins I'm seeing on the horizon? Well, maybe not, but I was certainly looking for them. Now it was 15 minutes before start-time. My constricting wetsuit was getting tighter, my breathing was becoming more pronounced. I've never swum that far before. This is nuts! My palms were sweaty. Shake the negative thoughts and think positive. Thinking, thinking . . . well, I didn't puke yet on the guy next to me, which is good. Why hadn't I just had that 4th baby, instead of signing up for this madness?

Ten minutes left. The professional athletes were sent on their way. By now the crowd had thickened, and there was a sea of 2,000 of us, beginning to huddle closer as the start time drew nearer. It was daunting to watch the professionals. If I was watching this event as a spectator, I would have taken the time to appreciate their grace and athleticism. Instead, it only churned up my sense of fear. The large swells of water seemed to swallow them up, as they swam out, becoming smaller and smaller. The music was loud, and the announcer was amusing the crowd with fun facts and comments. Would I feel it immediately if a shark bit my leg off or chomped me in half? My breathing became more shallow, and my suit became even more constricting. Darn, why do they have to make those collars so tight, anyway?

The announcer asked if there were any first-time Ironman athletes in the crowd. "Woo hoo!" many of us screamed. The crowd welcomed us with a roar of applause.

The time FINALLY arrived. 10, 9, 8 (oh please don't let me drown), 7, 6, (crap I can't believe I'm doing this), 5, 4, (there are too many people standing in my space!), 3, 2...the crowd yelled and cheered! I... stood there . . .

A powerful flow of athletes slipped past — it was like standing in a sea of lava. The crowd was pushing forward to the water. I, however, managed to weasel my way towards the back, by letting people slip by. Knowing I needed to face my fear, I let myself be led like a magnet behind the rest of the crowd. My toes hit the water . . . **wait, I am *not* a swimmer.**

Try not. Do or do not. There is no try.

—Yoda in the Empire Strikes Back

CHAPTER 6

I Am *Not* a Runner!

Four years earlier, I couldn't run two blocks. Seriously, I couldn't run. I *hated* it. I was *not* a runner. I weighed over 220 lbs. and felt my body was just not made to run.

Even though I hated running, I liked that it was going to help me lose weight. I joined Weightwatchers - four months later and 60 lbs. lighter (I'd gained some back by the time Ironman rolled around), I did my first six-mile run with a friend. I had worked myself into a tizzy before the run, as I was so nervous and uptight. My stomach actually churned when I thought of the scheduled run on the day before. I felt victorious completing that sixth mile.

I decided, right there and then, that I wanted to do a full marathon. What the heck? If I did six miles, I could do 26.2 miles, I thought. So, I signed up for Grandma's Marathon which was being held in Duluth, Minnesota, and was only six months from then. It was a pretty big event and hosted over 10,000 runners.

Training was a bit tougher than I had anticipated. It seemed so easy on paper to look at 26.2 miles and say sure, sign me up. The actual training was a bit different than it looked on paper! There were many times I questioned myself — what the heck was I doing?

My husband and kids were my sources of encouragement and inspiration. When Bob said I was going to complete it, no problem, it made me believe it, too. I believed in him, and he believed in me. Whenever a twinge of negativity crept in, knowledge of his belief would push me right through those times of uncertainty.

Six months had come incredibly fast. My body had held up pretty well during training and I was elated to have run up to 20 miles for my longest run at this point. I still didn't care much for running, but I loved what it did for me physically and mentally. Having something to train for was addictive and I enjoyed it very much. The thought of having the marathon come and go made me a little sad. I liked having a goal to shoot for and I liked that each day would hold a new challenge.

Several days before the marathon, I had heard of a local triathlon making its debut in our town in six weeks. I wanted to know more about what it involved. I thought it might be fun to have a new challenge and goal to train for. I knew a triathlon involved running, biking, and swimming, but wasn't even sure which order they were done in. So, I bought a few books to read on the subject.

The time had come for the big event. So, with three young kids in the van, we drove two hours to Duluth where Grandma's Marathon would be held the next day.

On the ride up to Duluth for the marathon, I was immersed in triathlon reading material. "Bob," I announced, "I want to do a triathlon in six weeks." There was complete silence. I noted a slight frown

starting to hover over his eyebrows. I was waiting for him to tell me I could do this. He'd always
been enthusiastic about my adventures in the
past, and I was a little baffled by his silence. After
15 years of marriage, he knew my overanxious,
obsessive nature of wanting to jump feet-first into
some new adventure. He had always been support-
ive and I wondered at his hesitation about this new
idea.

"Jen," he said cautiously, "Do you even know how to
swim?" I thought about it for a second. "Of *course* I
know how to swim," I said, with a dismissive wave
of my hand. "I took lessons as a kid." He simply
nodded, and didn't question me further. Hearing
no further inquiry or opposition, I interpreted his
silence to mean "Go for it!"

On the morning of the marathon, 10,000 of us
stood around in the heat, nervously waiting around
for the start. When the gun went off, we were ready.
Those first few miles were a blast. I was working
hard to pace myself and not rush ahead. I knew a
marathon was not at all like an all-out sprint. I'd
read something a few days before about how most
people hit a "wall" around mile 19 . . . it said, "This
is where the true race really starts." This helped me
to mentally prepare for miles 18–19 when I was
starting to hit my "wall." I kept thinking, "This is
where the race really starts." While I am not a fast

runner, I started to pick up the pace, while many runners around me were starting to slow down. As each mile crept by, bringing me closer to the finish line, I kept running a little faster even though, temperature wise, it was one of the hottest Grandma's marathons ever. Throughout the whole event, Bob and the kids, along with my brother Chuck, found me at several mile markers. It was a joy to look for them, and I enjoyed watching the kids get excited as they would join in and run along with me, here and there.

As I came to the last mile, I knew I had this running thing in the bag. The last few blocks, I ran as fast as I could. It was a thrill but I was a little shocked to find that the finish line ended up to be a bit further away then I'd thought. My heart was pounding as my feet flew across the finish line, just a little over four hours after I'd started. When I looked at my heart rate monitor, it read 205 beats per minute — the highest I had ever seen (I normally tried to train at around 150 or so). I couldn't quite hear anything for the first few minutes or so after finishing, but I was on cloud nine. I'd actually completed a marathon!

Shortly after Grandma's, I started training for my first sprint triathlon (.25 mile swim, 20 mile bike and a 3.1 mile run). I bought an $800 road bike. Really? Something with 2 wheels, a chain, and a set of handlebars — without a motor — costs $800? You bet it could, I soon discovered. I had an acute case of sticker shock, especially when I heard this was on the low end of road bikes!

The secret of getting ahead
is getting started.

—MARK TWAIN

CHAPTER 7

I Think I Can?

Two weeks before my first triathlon, I went to the beach for my first open water swim. Up until now, I had only swum a few times at our local community pool. With being at the beach, I wasn't worried about getting hit by boats. No big whoop. I would just swim a few laps and be done. It was only me and two other people there — the lifeguard looked bored. With my feet still touching the ground, I put my face in the water. Then, something unexpected happened. I started to hyperventilate. My head popped up. Huh, that is weird, I wonder what just happened? I looked around with an embarrassed grin. Did anyone see what I just did? Nope. I tried it again. Face in, feet firmly planted in the sandy bottom. Pure panic set in, as I felt like I couldn't breathe under water. Oh, you have GOT to be kidding! I looked around again . . . no one noticed me taking these ragged short breaths, did they? Jeepers creepers, I was only in waist-high water. You mean

I could do this as a kid, but now, as an adult, I've developed a fear of swimming in a lake?

The next day, I asked some of our friends' teenage daughters to take me to the beach. The goal? Swim to the buoys. I instructed the girls to let me look at their faces the whole way, and talk to me as we swam out. I promised I wouldn't reach out to them, as I just needed to be able to concentrate on their face and voices.

Fear started to set in as we swam beyond where our feet touched. I concentrated on their faces as I side-stroked farther out, trying not to think about the water being over my head. The girls chit-chatted the whole way out. Before we knew it, we had reached the buoys. We did it! The girls and I were screaming and laughing! During those moments of exuberance, while treading water, I never let on about my secret fear of losing one of my feet to a cold-blooded aquatic vertebrate with scales and gills, lurking below the surface. (Remember that scene in Jaws, when he took the person down by the buoys? To this day, I can't go near a buoy.)

Here I stood, three years later, at the start of my first Ironman competition. I was now up to my waist in salt water. I was playing it safe, staying towards the back of the swarm of bodies around me. The crowd of swimmers, all heading out in one mass was pretty scary- it was like a huge, churning, washing machine. I wanted no part of getting caught up in the rough action. Getting kicked didn't bug me as much as getting swam over . . . that terrified me.

My suit was very tight as the salt water felt like it was crushing my body. I walked further into the swells. Darn, are these new goggles tight enough? I yanked and pulled. Then I yanked and pulled some more . . . **SNAP**! What just happened? I stood there in horror. I was standing chest-high in salt water and my goggle strap just broke with part of the strap being slung shot somewhere out into the Gulf. It was nowhere to be found! There was not even enough of the strap left to try to tie around my head. I questioned if I could swim without the goggles? The answer was no, not in salt water. Just the few drops that had trickled in my eyes already were enough to make me squint.

Time stood still. The waves swelled around me, but I could not hear or feel them. Complete silence. **THINK!**

I turned around and started to "water run" my way back to the beach. If I just yelled my request and waved my goggles around, surely someone would know what happened. It felt like I was in a fish bowl full of water trying to communicate to those outside of the glass. They couldn't hear me.

A broken goggle strap had the potential to ruin a year's worth of planning and training. Really? One stupid strap? I started to wave harder, yell louder, and "run" faster towards shore. Can anyone hear me? "I must look ridiculous, raving like some mad person," I thought. There I was, running toward the shore, while EVERY other athlete was already swimming the opposite way!

Ah, bless that remarkable announcer, as he spotted me. He knew what I was trying to say. "Get her some goggles from the lost and found," he shouted. I was smiling. He got it. A Good Samaritan tossed some goggles to me, and I tossed my broken pair back. I looked down, and found it to be a gift from God. Out of all the goggles in the world, these secondhand goggles were my favorite goggle style (Aqua Sphere Seal goggles), which were very difficult to find. I'd actually looked for this exact style at several shops in the past weeks and couldn't find them. They were well-worn, but they were the greatest goggles in the world to me at that minute (and still are today).

I turned around to go back out. The swells were huge. The other swimmers were quite a ways ahead of me. I started to wade out farther. Before long, I couldn't touch the bottom anymore. My breathing started to get ragged. Here we go. I started swimming. My chest got extremely tight and I couldn't breathe. Oh no, I was starting to hyperventilate. Out of the corner of my eye, I spotted a very concerned looking lifeguard watching over me. "Just act normal," I thought. There was *no way* that young kid was going to "save" me from drowning, as I had trained too hard and too long to quit at this point.

I must be swimming in 1,000 feet deep water by now . . . lots of ocean life below. My breathing was getting worse, and I started to swallow salt water. **Yuck!** It felt like my mouth was spray painted with sea salt.

Remember the kids' movie Nemo? Well, Dory's lighthearted voice from that movie kept playing over and over in my head, "Just keep swimming, keep on swimming." Stay calm. Sputter, sputter. Breathe.

Was that a shark coming straight at me from the murky depths? Was that a fin I just felt? Was a half-eaten leg going to come floating by me? Okay, I thought. Think positive. Negative thoughts will get you nowhere. Okay, here it goes, here is my most positive thought I can throw at myself at this exact second . . . What came to mind? It was the most positive thought I could come up with: If a shark bites me right now, I can end this madness. (I swear that is really what I thought.) That was as positive as I could get, as I was thrashing about.

The swells coming up now seemed like mountains to me. Where are the five-foot buoys? They were completely blocked from my view as each wave rose up. Dory's voice rang out in my head, "Just keep swimming, keep on swimming." I swallowed some more salt water. I can't breathe. This suit is too tight. Oh my gosh, someone just kicked me. *Breathe*!

The sun was right in our eyes, as it was coming up to greet this day. It was so beautiful, but very blinding, making it harder to sight the buoys. Swim, swim, *breathe*. Spit out salt water. Swim, swim, take a *gulp* of air *now*. Perhaps if I started to thrash about more with my arm, I would get this over sooner. Besides didn't thrashing about scare sharks away? Or did it signal dinner?

I rounded the first corner. I did it. Uh oh — now there were several more people rounding the corner . . . don't swim over me please! The first long rectangle length of the swim was completed. Did I really make it to the last buoy? I am still in one piece, all body parts accounted for, and I have not drowned. This is good. I am doing it. *I am swimming*! Turn the corner.

The sun was now at my back. "This is going to be lovely," I thought.

Oh no, what is coming at me like a wall? I strained to see . . . the professional swimmers were coming straight at me on their last lap. Swim! Swim faster! Get out of the way because they *will* swim over anything in their way, including *me*! These are some of the most powerful swimmers in the world. Thankfully, I was able to swim off to the far side, clear out of their way before the group roared past me.

I finally started to stretch my body out into long easy strides. The tension started to leave, my breathing slowed down, and I was actually calming down.

As I started to near the beach I was suddenly elated. I was almost done with the first of two 1.2 mile laps. I only had one more to go. This was the furthest distance I had ever swum before and now I was about to attempt to double it.

Standing up the last part of the lap left me a little dizzy. I scampered up to the beach. There were two paths. One was for the people that had finished their two laps and the other for the rest of us to go back in the water. Each path was crowded with people cheering. Would anyone notice if a slightly "larger- boned" athlete slid in behind the extremely trim, fit professional athletes that were taking the "done" path? "Can you guess what person doesn't fit in?" I thought. Yep, get back in the line to go back out for another lap.

I was still slightly dizzy, but was starting to feel on top of the world. I could do this. I just swam the farthest distance I had ever swum. I didn't drown, and haven't been eaten by a shark (yet). A good day so far!

Going back out for the second lap wasn't as scary now. I was going to do it. The waves weren't so large and the sun wasn't so blinding by this time. The water was still as salty (yuck) but my suit didn't feel as tight anymore. I relished reaching my arms out into long smooth strokes. I could breathe (yeaa!) and I wasn't looking for sharks as much on this lap. I was going to live (Yesss!) and I was going to finish this swim! The very thought filled me with joy.

The warmth from the bright sun felt like God was shining down on me. I relished being in His presence in the midst of doing something extraordinary.

My body stretched out farther and farther with each long stroke. My breathing and body were extremely relaxed. With each stroke, I knew it was drawing me closer and closer to the finish line.

It felt like I had sure come a long way from just a few months ago when my kids had been with me on some of my outdoor lake swims. It would literally take me 10–20 minutes to jump from the pontoon boat into our shallow lake on which we live in Minnesota. I had seen the big snapping turtles that would lay their eggs on our dirt road in the spring . . . I just knew I was going to get a few of my toes bitten off from one of those suckers. They were just biding their time waiting for me. Visions of their jaws would linger in my head as I would be standing on the edge of the boat trying to get up enough guts to jump in. The entire time I would say, "Okay, okay . . . okay, okay." In the background, my three kids and Bob would be chanting "*Go* mama go! *Jump* mama *jump!*" It wasn't until I could see Bob starting to lose patience that I would force myself to jump in. I literally hyperventilate the first few minutes with my head out of the water until I would tire myself out. It would then force my face in the water so I would have to start swimming.

After my first few smaller triathlons, I had come to accept that I have a fear of swimming outdoors. It was just something I had and needed to deal with. So, I wouldn't let myself think of this fear until my toes hit the starting line of each race. Each race it would be the same panicked feeling that would wear off when I forced myself to stop hyperventilating. It was what it was. I couldn't help it so I just dealt with it.

I knew I would have the same fear today, but not to this extent. Swimming in the large swells of the Gulf was completely different than swimming in a lake. I think that is probably why the feeling of accomplishment seemed so great. I was facing my fear head-on and just doing it.

I finally felt like a swimmer! I actually started to smile beneath the water. This was fun! I wasn't nearly as tired as I thought I would be. The adrenaline was carrying me towards the cheering crowds on the beach.

I finished the swim with a huge smile on my face. I was quite disoriented when I got out of the water, but I was feeling fantastic! For someone who always thought she wasn't a swimmer, this felt like an awesome accomplishment. I didn't care that I was one of the last ones out of the water. I'd finished within the allotted time limit. I shuffled my way across the beach while wonderful well-wishers congratulated me.

There are no secrets to success. It is the result of preparation, hard work, and learning from failure.

—Colin Powell

CHAPTER 8

I Am *Not* a Pro Cyclist!

Off to the "strippers." Yes, I said strippers. The strippers consisted of a group of young guys who totally took control and were in charge of getting those tight wetsuits off. You stood when and where they said to stand and they did the rest. One minute I was upright, and the next, this 185 pound body was flipped like a pancake and my wetsuit was off. Did I remember to wear a swim suit underneath? I briefly worried . . . Yes, no need for concern. Within a blink, I was standing upright again. Wow, was that ever fun! You couldn't help but laugh out loud.

A trip through the cold showers that were set up along the path, then a shuffle-run to a changing tent in the parking lot where the transition area was located.

The transition area is where all athletes transition from swimming to biking (called the T1 transition) and then from biking to running (called the

T2 transition). All gear is carefully packed (and repacked several times) by each athlete into what is called your transition bags. The bags along with your bicycle are dropped off the day before the event and then lined up by your bib number. When the athletes come in to the transition area from their swim and run portions, volunteers will call out your bib number and grab your transition bag with your gear packed into it. In the midst of the transition area is a large white tent that is divided into a male and female tent. Athletes will get geared up for their next event in these tents and leave their transition bags to be picked up after the event.

The transition area is quite a sight to see with the large tent, all the 2,000+ bikes carefully lined up and the transition bags all in numerical order in a penned off area. If you want to see some of the world's most expensive bikes, just visit an Ironman sometime. You are bound to see the most expensive and fastest bikes around.

Here, I was met by two wonderful volunteer angels, who sorted everything I'd packed in my transition bag. They were so kind and excited to help. I felt like one of my kids, getting dressed for the first day of school. Off with the swimsuit, on with my clothes. They even put on my shoes and made sure my watch was strapped on properly. They were both here as volunteers for the event and planned to sign up for next year's event.

I rushed out the tent door, and was stopped by more of these great volunteers, waiting for each person to come out. In their hands were roasting pans filled with chunky globs of white suntan lotion, just waiting to be slathered on each swimmer-turned-biker. And when I say one is slathered, I mean they coated on the suntan lotion. I felt like a corn on the cob at the State Fair (where several of them once worked). It was great.

Off now to find my bike. One benefit to being one of the last ones out of the water was that there weren't many bikes left. The volunteers yell out your bib number as you are going to your bike, then someone gets it ready for you. A very kind volunteer had a bike ready to go for me. "No," I shook my head," That isn't my bike.." He looked at my number, then back to me and nodded his head, smiling. Yes, it was mine. I didn't want to be rude, but I said, "No," and waved my hand no to indicate he grabbed the wrong one. He smiled and nodded. When I got to the bike, lo and behold, it really *was* mine. The volunteer had a big grin on his face and we laughed. I guess all of that salt water had drained me of some brain cells, or maybe I was giddy at having survived the swim . . . ? Probably both!

Now, off to the bike ride. Yesss. My longest ride up to this point was 96 miles. Bring it on. This was definitely my favorite part of the triathlon. The morning was still a bit cool, and I was chilled from being in the water. I didn't care. It was heaven to be sitting on that bike, where I would *get* to ride 112 miles. How blessed was I?

My blissful state of mind changed quickly to one of concern, when the wind became a major force for the first half of the ride. Attempting to pedal forward with Mother Nature pushing against you is really exhausting. One had to just hunker down as best they could, and pedal, pedal, and pedal some more through the 112 mile single-loop course.

While riding, I had plenty of time to reflect back on the past year. I thanked God many times on that ride for the beauty that surrounded me, for my friends and their encouragement, and for allowing me to physically be here, doing this. I especially thanked Him for my *awesome* husband and three kids for sacrificing time away from me to let me train for this day.

I also reflected on the biking crew that I had trained with. They were a fun, yet quirky group of guys that were in their 40s and 50s. They were very strong bikers, and were patient about mentoring me through the finer points of biking. I was the only female in the group and I think they were a bit shocked at the volume of chatter I can generate, especially while riding. Up until I'd arrived, they probably hadn't said more than a handful of words to each other on any given bike ride. This dedicated pack of bikers taught me to pace myself, to take in fluids regularly, and to pedal smoothly rather than mash my foot pedals down. They also mentored me on the particulars of riding with a group. I still cringe when recalling some lessons learned in that department.

One of those learning moments took place during a Multiple Sclerosis fundraising benefit about a year after I started riding with the group. The MS150 is a two-day ride where people of all ages and backgrounds take part. It was the first time I had ever been away from my kids for an overnight stay, which was a huge deal to me. The two-day ride was beyond awesome, and I felt very strong during and after the 75 miles we rode each day. Our group was a bit competitive, and we were among the first to arrive at our destination each day.

You have to know the whole picture to fully appreciate this story: My awesome group of biking gurus are very kind, sweet, bike snobs. Their bikes are always well kept. Maintenance, cleanliness, and attention to detail during any transport was a priority. They were well-versed in all of the written and unwritten rules and nuances of biking. Each and every trek included a detailed route map. I, on the other hand, was still learning, and thought judging my location on a route could easily be accomplished by noting an occasional restaurant marker. I had no use for a map, as I had their back tires for my map. I just followed along, and didn't really care where we went, just as long as we got to ride. In my world, my bike was considered clean if I had cleaned it in the last year. I took my share of razzing about this. I'm certain they would have preferred I take some of that constructive criticism a little more to heart.

So, here we were, on this MS150 ride. Our two-day, 150-mile ride was coming to a close. All in all, an exhilarating time, that is, until we neared the finish line. People were along the route, cheering and ringing cowbells. The finish line was in view. We only had a few blocks left to go.

I remember our friend Walt saying, "Hey, let's ride in side-by-side, so we can get some great pictures of us coming in as a team at the finish line." Great, we all thought. So we lined up our bikes, side-by-side, to ride the last two or so blocks.

There were about 10 of us and from the pictures it looked pretty impressive to see us all arriving in one united front. Most of the team worked for a very prestigious construction and building manage-ment company, and we had their company name and logo proudly plastered across our bright yellow team shirts. Up until this point in my short biking career, I had only learned how to ride with a pack of riders in a single-file line.

The announcer was commenting as we appeared, saying how great we looked, and making a big deal out of the fact that we had all lined up to come in as a team. The cowbells were ringing and the crowd was cheering. I am cringing at the thought of what happens next.

I am a bit clumsy, and always have been. I try to be graceful when possible, but sometimes it just doesn't work. It comes as no surprise that I wasn't named something like Willow, Lily, Petunia, or Daisy.

Enough stalling, I suppose . . . .Well, there I was, riding along in a straight line and doing just fine, until I started to feel claustrophobic with these bikes on either side of me. This was new to me, as I had only ridden with bikes behind and in front of me before. I concentrated, doing my best to keep going straight, and started to tense up. Just go straight and for cripes sake, DON'T panic! What if I . . . No, just . . . go . . . straight! Then it happened, out of nervous tension, I felt my bike give the smallest of jerks, and I let my handle bars give a small jerk. It happened in the blink of an eye and that smallest, slightest jerk of my handle bars made my tires bump into Walt's bike next to me.

What happened next was like a slow, unfolding nightmare. I started to lose my balance! I was trying to stay upright, but the only way I could was to lean into the person next to me while I pedaled fast and furious, attempting to regain my balance. By this time, it was too late. My body weight had caused me to totally lean over, right into Walt.

In slow motion, I heard my fellow biker yell, "Jen, what the heck are you doing?" "I am *so sorrrrrreeeee!*" I yelled, as I was now fully leaning on Walt, as I'd lost all ability of holding myself up. In turn, Walt began to fall sideways, too! It was like watching human dominos on bikes! The *whole* team proceeded to fall over, *one...by...one.* The announcer and the crowd gasped. The scene was unfolding before me in slow motion, and I looked on in horror, as each of my teammates went down, one . . . by . . . one . . . by . . . one, *right at* the finish line.

To make matters worse, the whole thing was caught in photos . . . frame by painful frame. The first picture shows us looking like a group of professionals, all lined up perfectly. The next frame shows me leaning over towards Walt. Then the next set document the whole agonizing chain of events — one rider being knocked down, then the next, and so on . . . until most of the team lay on the pavement, with the astonished and concerned crowd in the background.

The last picture was of Walt and Ross — the ones who'd arranged the whole event for the team. They had designed the shirts, gained us entry into the event, arranged where we would stay, etc. The picture showed Walt with this bewildered look on his face, walking with Ross, who also looked bewildered, and quite dazed. In Ross' hand, he carried the tire that had broken off the new expensive road bike he was so proud of.

I was *beyond* horrified at what had just happened. No amount of apologies could take back that slight jerk that had caused the whole fiasco. To make matters worse, one of our team members was tossed from her bike and injured her wrist. The close-knit team that had banded together for the past 48 hours had disbanded entirely. One by one, they all scattered with shocked, astonished expressions on their faces.

I was devastated to have caused such a horrific accident. Alan, who was the only triathlete out of the group and appreciated a good chit chat on a bike ride, walked me to where we had parked. I was stunned, dazed and in disbelief at what just happened. He looked over at me and said, "What a great weekend." I couldn't believe it. Had he not just been involved with this disaster only minutes earlier? "Alan," I said, "I just knocked down the *whole* team at the finish line. I was the cause of people getting injured!" He looked at me with a grin and repeated, "Jen, that was a great weekend wasn't it?" *Hello*, did you not hear what I said? "Alan, I knocked the whole team down!" I said louder, shaking my head as tears started to well up. "Jen," he said louder as he looked at me with a stern smile, "It *was* a great weekend!" He wasn't getting it (really, I wasn't), so I just nodded and said, "Yeah, I guess it was."

I felt awful and was in tears afterwards. When I got home, I broke out in tears again when Bob cheerfully asked me how it went. Tears from wanting to take back the last few blocks of the ride fell as I told him what had happened. He felt terrible for me, but said not to worry about it and that it would blow over.

The next day my boss was excited to hear about it how it went. I choked out the whole story of what happened. He was nearly in tears by the time I was done telling the story. He was laughing so hard, he was crying, when I finished my tale of woe, he blurted out, "You are so clumsy McDoo. Only you could knock down a whole construction team." I cracked a smile from my teary eyes, as I knew he was right!

The next weekend, I ran my second ever full marathon which was again Grandma's in Duluth (it would be again another scorcher of a marathon in terms of heat). I was elated to have completed it with a friend of mine that I had gotten to train with from work. We both would do our training runs before work, around 5:00 A.M. However, no matter how great it was to complete my second marathon, I still felt bad about what happened the week before when I got back together with my biking crew.

Rather than receiving the razzing I rightly deserved, my biking crew showed me there was another side to them when I went biking with them the week following the marathon.

I wanted NOTHING to do with riding within 10 feet of any other biker again. I believed my bike crew must have sensed this. Shortly into the ride, these folks embraced my presence, made me feel at ease by chatting it up, demonstrated their forgiveness, and by gracing me with a dozen roses to congratulate me for my accomplishment the week before. Their thoughtfulness and friendship meant a great deal to me, and I am forever grateful to have found such a wonderful group of people to share this part of my journey.

It was quite some time before I could talk about it without getting upset however. Now when I think of that memory, I still cringe, but can laugh about it and chalk it up as one of those great lessons learned.

As I grow older I pay less
attention to what men say.
I just watch what they do.

—ANDREW CARNEGIE

CHAPTER 9

Stay Focused?

While I love to bike, there were many times during the year that I struggled to train. With the Minnesota weather, most people here wrap up their serious training in September. Come September, the roads tend to be pretty desolate without so many people training. No bikers are found on the quiet rural roads. A few serious runners are still out training for the early October marathons, but even that drops off suddenly after the first of October. I missed seeing other people out training.

The last three months or so of bike training were mentally and physically tough for me. Towards fall, the weather turned unseasonably cold and gloomy. It seemed to rain a lot and at times it felt like slivers of ice pelting my face. I was tired and less patient with those around me, including my family. Every day of those last few weeks, I was just plain tired. I was more irritated by little things, and there *never* seemed to be enough time for sleep. On a handful of weekdays I allowed myself to sleep until 5:30 A.M. It was sheer luxury. Could I have slept in every day and trained at night? Yes, I probably could have, but that would have meant shirking my responsibilities as a wife and mother. If I was going to do this, I had to maintain the discipline to yank myself out of bed and just do it.

It was a time of extreme discipline and focus that few will ever understand. Anyone can get through those easy fun days . . . it is those difficult training days that were a test for me. They are the ones where my patience, discipline, perseverance, and faith in myself and in my plan are tested. Would I even be able to complete the distance? On great days, I would confidently believe that by sticking to my training program, I would have a good chance. On days I was exhausted, feeling down, and/or just having a rough training session, my confidence level sunk low. It was during these times that my magnificent husband was there to push me through. His confidence in me never wavered, and he was always there to confide to me that he knew I could do this. I will always be grateful to him for his love and patience with me throughout this journey. He knew I was going to make it. I hoped I was going to make it.

On one of my last long training rides, it started to snow. I had a five hour ride to complete and the sleet and rain felt like sharp razors on my exposed skin.

Tough it out I thought, just do it. After an hour of riding, I physically couldn't do it. My thin bike tires were slipping and sliding on the wet pavement. Part of my body was numb from the cold, and the parts I *could* feel hurt from the jades of slush pelting at me. When I pulled up to the house, Bob was there waiting for me. I started to cry. There was no way I could ride 4 hours on a stationary bike trainer. An hour, possibly 90 minutes was my max. I couldn't do it. If I stopped, I would have felt defeated for not accomplishing my goal that day. Being that it was one of my last long rides, it was an important training session.

My bike was resting on the stationary trainer. I couldn't do it I defeatedly cried. If I were Bob, I would have said something like, "Maybe another day, honey, just relax for now." He knew me too well. Instead, he quietly put in a movie for us to watch, and turned up the volume so I could hear it over the noise of the trainer spinning with my back wheel. He smiled and said quietly, "You can do this." I looked longingly back outside. I couldn't face being on a trainer for four hours. For me, this was a daunting task, mentally and physically. When you bike outside, you have the ever-changing scenery to keep your mind occupied. Going up and down hills affords some rest, as you can allow yourself to glide some of the way. Being on the trainer is a constant pedal motion. The seat always seemed harder on my rear end when I was stuck on a trainer. The movie started, and as I started to pedal, I sucked in the last few sniffles and allowed those last few tears from fatigue and frustration to dry on my cheeks.

Four hours later, the training session was complete. It definitely wasn't my favorite session, but looking back, it makes me smile to think of my husband's quiet encouragement and ability to know exactly what I needed. It felt like we were in this together.

On my long 4–6 hour rides, I cherished the times that the weather was great. God seemed to be one with me on those beautiful rides. Time and time again I thanked Him for letting me do this. Life really slowed down for these workouts and I felt very close to Him. It was usually the highlight of my training sessions to get to bike.

Not all the long rides were lovely though. My longest training ride took place just three weeks before the event. I rode 95 miles in six hours with an hour run afterwards. I rode the first five hours in sleeting rain — another *cold* and lonely bike ride. The wind was pretty wicked and it was hard to hear. By the fifth hour, my toes were completely numb and I felt like it was one of the most miserable times in my life.

For the last half hour of the ride, the sun came out. My negative attitude shifted and I was reminded once again of how very blessed and fortunate I was. When all was said and done, I was very proud to have pushed through the pain and misery so I could enjoy the final reward.

Training sessions like these were physically and mentally tough, yet they honed my skills of endurance and perseverance for sports and life. I learned to just get through the bad sessions the best I could, and not to dwell on what could have or should have been. I've learned to face life's challenges like they were my last-ever training session, and remind myself how very blessed I am for having the chance to do this.

My body was being taxed with the long training sessions and my immune system was running low. One week after the rainy 95-mile ride, I started to get sick. A few days later, just 3 weeks to Ironman, my journal entry reads, *"Probably most sick in adult life. Sick of sweating while sleeping. Sleeping just about entire time — kids are being so good. Bob sick too."*

I was sick for almost two weeks! Not only was I sicker than I could ever remember, but there was no way I could train at all.

Just eight days out from Ironman, I remembered being so relieved to be getting better, but I was still weak. I felt panicked to have lost almost two weeks of training, especially so close to the event.

The first morning back at the pool, I happily jumped in for my 5:30 A.M. swim. It was nice to start to feel normal again. I started my first lap, and savored it as I felt like I was "gliding" down the pool — Wow, isn't this great! That "gliding" feeling only lasted until halfway down the first length — then I started coughing and sputtering. I couldn't get enough air. My body had failed me.

I got out of the pool feeling depressed and sick. The 18-year-old or so lifeguard came up to me while I was soaking in the hot tub. "Are you okay madam?" he politely asked with a concern. Oh my gosh, I had an Ironman event in eight days, I couldn't even swim one length of the pool and now, apparently, I was a "madam"? I wanted to scream, "*No*, I'm *not* okay!" Instead, I just smiled and nodded that I was.

Slowly, my strength and endurance started to come back. It was only four days before the event when I was finally able to run again. However, I still wasn't able to breathe right in the pool. I was pretty weak.

Don't find fault.
Find a remedy.

—HENRY FORD

CHAPTER 10

All Systems Go!

Three days before the event, my husband and I packed our three kids, my brother Chuck, and my "tri bike" into our van, and drove 23 hours to Florida. Bob had become very ill during the days leading up to our trip. He was so sick, but didn't complain. He and my brother drove most of the way.

After the long 23-hour drive, we finally arrived. The kids did great. We had given each of them a $10 roll of quarters and told them it was theirs to keep. The only caveat was that anytime we heard a complaint or a "when are we going to be there" type of whine on the way down, we would take 25 cents from their stash. By gosh, it was the best $30 we ever spent! Only one quarter was taken away during the entire trip. Robbie, our 7 year-old analytical one of the bunch just couldn't help himself. Near the end of the drive, he had to ask, "Are we almost there yet?" in a whiny tone, just 10 miles from our hotel. He was outraged to have to pay his dues. The other two were snickering as the quarter was passed up to the front of the van. They chuckled even more as we talked about how we were going to spend that quarter — Rob sulked quietly in the back.

Overall, they did great! It took 23 hours for them to earn that money, and only about 30 minutes for them to blow it all at a video arcade we found in town.

Once settled into our temporary quarters, I wanted nothing more than to shop around and take in all the sights and sounds of the event, but I needed to rest. Kevin, a friend who'd done several Ironman competitions warned me to stay away from other athletes, explaining that it would drain me. I realized what he meant. The anxiety level at the hotel was very high, and I was careful to shield myself.

It was the night before the race, and it was also Halloween. I just wanted to rest and veg out, but poor Bob was so ill. The kids . . . well they were kids. At ages 8, 7, and 6, it was Halloween, and it didn't matter to them that it was only hours from the moment in time where my efforts from an entire year would finally come to fruition. It was Ironman Eve. As a mom, I knew it didn't matter either. So, we packed them up after dinner, and had them dress up with very homemade costumes. Max and Maggie dressed as runners (they had my running hats, tennis shoes, shirts on), and Robbie was a football player (he had my bike gloves and a jacket on). Some children have professional, ornate and detailed costumes — my kids went with creative! They were so proud of their costumes, and I was humbled at that moment to be their mom. I was so proud of them. They had a blast, and after only 40 minutes they were ready to go back to the room. I was the one that wanted to stay out; perhaps it was a good distraction — their joy was rejuvenating!

The next day, as I rode that 112 miles, I felt like I was flying. Other than the powerful wind, the weather was perfect and 90% of the roads were accommodating. I passed the time by praying, giving thanks, letting my thoughts wander, and "catching" other riders. It was fun to focus in on a rider and work to pass them. Because I was one of the last swimmers to get out, I was able to pass several hundred cyclists. It was like a game of tag. Zero in, catch, and then find another one.

Thankfully, I went through the bike portion with no flat tires.

Several times on the ride, I had a van full of cheering family screaming and yelling words of encouragement to me. Leave it to my husband, even as sick as he was, to make an all-out effort to find me. To me, all bikers look pretty much the same. I don't know how he does it, but he always finds me in any race. Wow, how I cherished getting to see those little faces smiling and yelling out the window. The hours on the bike flew by, and I relished most of it.

Remember, I am not a runner.

As mentioned earlier, I started off running several years before making the decision to enter the Ironman. While I had run 3 marathons since, I still didn't consider myself a runner. I enjoy watching those people that run like they are floating. You know who I'm talking about. Those people who make it appear as though running is a primary purpose in life . . . their stride as swift, effortless and fluid as a gazelle, their feet barely hitting the road as they glide forward, barely hearing the sound of their breath. They have a look of contentment on their face — they are the true runners. I, on the other hand, consider myself a "sled runner." I look like I am tired of running from the start with a "Let's get this over with" look on my face. My blocky style, while slow, does me well on long distance runs, however. In longer running events, those gazelles often look like me. I figure in the end, we all even out and look the same anyway, so it didn't bug me to be a sled-type runner.

Fast forward to the present.

Here I was. I was not a swimmer, but on this day, I swam my longest distance. I also did my longest bike ride ever, and now I was just a mere 26.2 miles away from becoming an Ironman. A whole marathon and I'm done . . .

Getting off the bike after being on it for 6 ½ hours was a little tough. My butt felt glued to the seat. My body was not moving with any fluidity. Trying to dismount my bike, I most closely resembled a pre-lube version of the Tin Man.

Now, off to another changing tent. Thanks to the wonderful volunteers helping me, I was able to move my limbs enough to get dressed in some fresh clothes. When I emerged from the tent, I was doused with another layer of sunscreen.

Off I went. The crowd cheered as we emerged from the transition area out into the two lap running course. My legs felt like they had cement blocks attached to them. Thankfully, I had experienced this sensation many times while training, only here, I was too prideful to grimace. Wave, smile, and "run." When I say run, it was more like trying to move your feet in a forward motion, through fast-drying cement. Nevertheless, I was still was grinning ear to ear. Two events done. One to go. And I have done this part before! Life was good.

I was keeping an eye out for my family, but hadn't seen them since hours earlier, while cycling. I missed them, but was hoping they were having a good time, whatever they were doing. I found out later that parts of the running course was closed to vehicles, so Bob and Chuck took the kids fishing for a few hours before they took up near the finish line to anxiously await my arrival.

The first five or so miles were *great*. I was still high on the fact that the swim and bike portions were behind me.

I was clipping along, and found a very good running companion for the first few miles. My new-found friend had said this was his second Ironman event, and he was excited to be here. He, too, had kids and we talked about the joy of being able to train with and around our families. We both agreed that we were also looking forward to life slowing down and things returning to "normal."

The volunteer support was incredible. We were treated like royalty. Every mile there was a team of volunteers that had drinks and nourishment. To this day, I am ever thankful for the care and kindness shown to us by these dedicated volunteers. Each mile, I looked forward to seeing another smiling face that was eager to help. I was sure to thank each and every person I could. They were amazing.

A day before the event, families were invited to create their own personal 2x2 ft sign for their favorite athletes. Each sign had handwritten notes and drawings. These signs of encouragement were displayed about every four miles (so you would see the signs around miles 4, 8, 16, and 20). I smiled as I found the sign my kids made for me. It was plopped amidst a virtual collage of hundreds of signs. I missed my husband and was hopeful to see my brother and kids soon.

The sign made me feel my kids were with me, cheering me on. I wasn't sure where they were and realized that among a sea of over 2,000 athletes, it was quite possible that we simply didn't see each other. Still, I saw their sign and at that moment, it was sufficient to sustain my momentum. I felt truly blessed God let me find it!

I chuckle as I remembered a few of the sayings our kids had written: Go Mama. Your #1. 1st Pies (meaning 1st place). You will win Mama. My favorite was "Don't Quet." Yes, spelled "Quet." My kids went to a Spanish immersion school, and their English spelling was awful. I smiled and thought, "You bet I won't QUET, my little love bugs!"

After mile 5, the novelty of running was starting to wear off. The support stations that were *only* a mile apart up until this point seemed to be getting farther apart. Are you kidding, I haven't come to the volunteer station yet? I am tired. My smiles became less enthusiastic.

I am a soda snob. I can't stand flat soda pop. I won't drink from a soda bottle that has been open for more than 15 minutes, as I believe it starts to go flat. I love the fizz! Flat cola was one of the options at the volunteer stations. Why on earth would anyone want to drink flat cola, I wondered? I gave in and decided to try some, as I could feel my body starting to lose energy. I needed sugar. Oh, if only the pop was fizzy I thought. Well, I got my wish. One of the sodas I drank had a bit of fizz in it. Several steps later I looked like a rabid dog — my mouth was filled with foam! It kept coming up and foaming out. Ah, now I understood the need for flat pop.

Around mile 6, I was starting to rely on that flat pop, as I could feel my body depleting itself of energy. By mile 7, it was starting to get a little chilly. The sun was starting to dim as nighttime approached. Ah . . . the next volunteer station had hot chicken broth. I never tasted anything so good. I was now addicted to flat cola and chicken broth. I tried to shove some bananas down, but it was a lot of effort for my body to try to process solid food.

At mile 8, I saw the kids' sign again. I read their writings and smiled. This time, the "Don't Quet" saying that my daughter Maggie had written stood out. My body was definitely starting to shut down and each mile felt like 10. I hadn't seen my family since early on in the bike portion of this endurance test and I was starting to lose confidence and hope. I needed them. I wanted to see their little faces and hear Bob's confident voice. I wanted to see my brother who had braved the trip down with us. Where were they? I trudged on, but I was starting to slow down considerably.

Once you learn to quit, it becomes a habit.

—Vince Lombardi

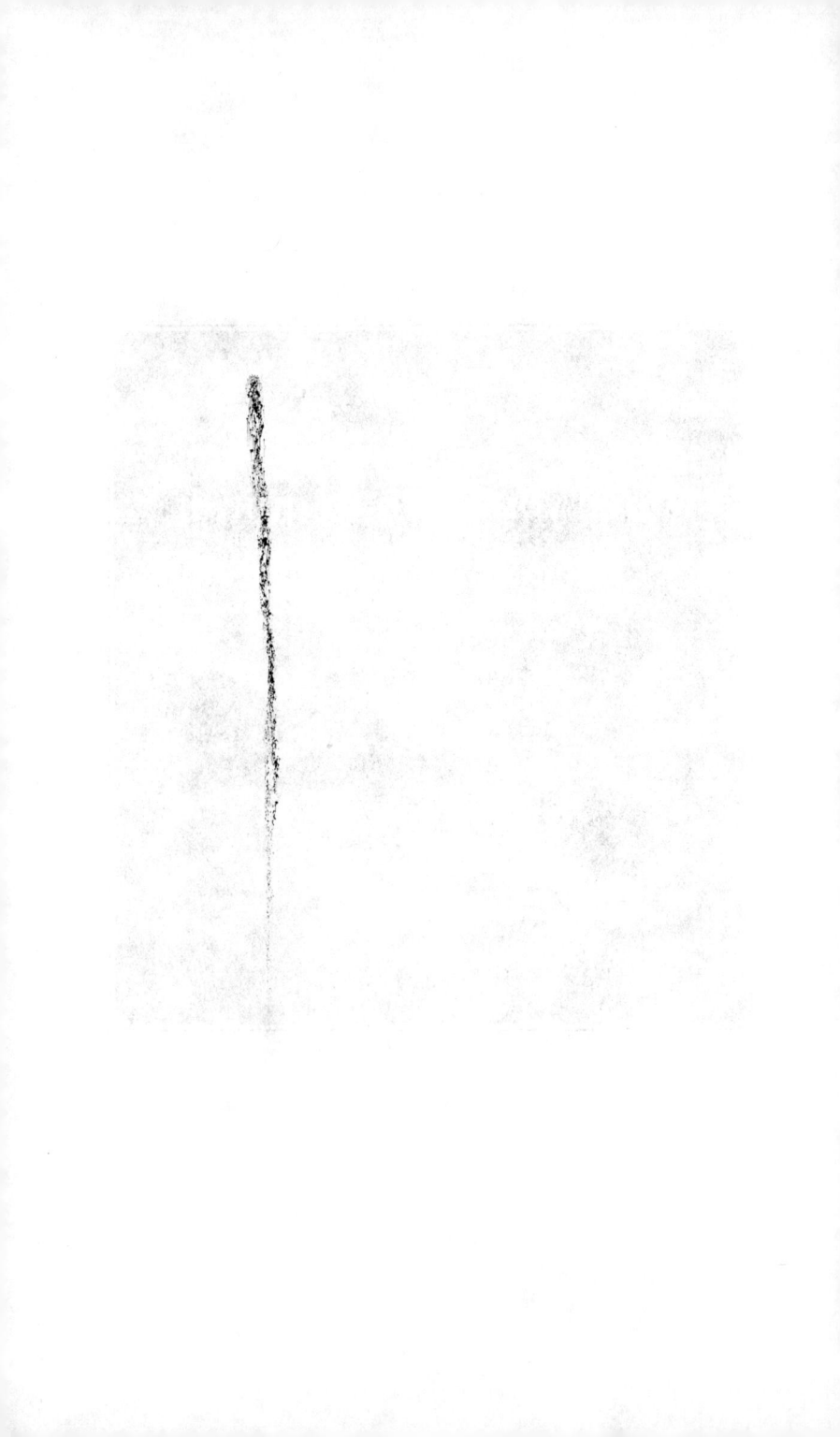

CHAPTER 11

I Quet!

It is said that competing in an Ironman event is filled with a lifetime of emotions. So far, I had felt *many* that day . . . thankfully most of them were positive.

This journey had started one year before when I was excited to have gotten an entry into the event. One year later, here I was. Almost every hour of every day I thought about this day. What would it be like? Could I do it? Was my plan the right one? Was I crazy for attempting to do this? I am not a swimmer. I am not a runner. I'm not really an endurance-type person. Only athletes do this, right? I was a mom and wife, not a "real" athlete. Was this worth the sacrifice? Would I be able to finish? At least the sharks didn't get me.

I had not really slept well the night before the event. I had awakened at 2:00 A.M. and drifted in and out of sleep, until I got up at 4:15 A.M. Now, some

12 hours after the 7:00 A.M. start gun went off, here I was, still on the course, running. My body had been drenched and dried over and over again with sweat. I could taste the salt that had formed on the outside of my mouth.

I was getting exhausted, both physically and emotionally, beyond anything I had ever felt in my life. Where was my family? I really needed them. I was starting to lose it mentally and physically. I tried to say a prayer of thanks, but even my faith was starting to waiver. I was starting not to care about finishing.

The blaring music from the finish line could be heard from a few miles away. As I got closer, the cheers from the crowd could be heard as others were finishing their journey. I started to slow a little more. I knew I was only hitting the half-way point.

As I neared the finish line, there were two directions to go. Straight ahead, the road led towards the cheering crowd and onto the finish line. This is where the runners only had about .2 miles left to the finish line. I could feel it, hear it, and taste it. It was *right* there. Then, there was the path off to the left that held the turnaround point for the rest of us. It felt like a punishment to have to swerve left around that cone instead of going straight to the finish line.

It was at that exact moment that my hope vanished, and I hit the lowest point of the day. It wasn't just low, it was lower than low. It was getting dark out. The crowd was getting thick with onlookers and people cheering. The blaring music and people cheering was incredible but a bit overwhelming for my already taxed psyche.

I had *over* 13 miles left to go. It was then that I almost came to a complete stop.

All day, I had been ticking off the miles and counting them down. I *only* had this many miles to go. Then the next miles left me *only* with this many miles and so on. I would silently give a cheer to myself thinking I am going to do this. I am going to become an **Ironman**!

This method was working up until this point. All of sudden, life sucked. This event sucked. I sucked. I wanted out. I hurt like I never hurt before. I was exhausted, and I hadn't seen my family for most of the day. I wanted out! The change of attitude happened like a light switch turning off. Instead of thinking I was already to the halfway point with *only* about 13.2 miles left, I let a whiny voice in my head tell me that I still had too far to go, that I was too tired and that I still had a half-marathon left to do! A little over 13 freaking miles left to go!

It was now getting cooler, as the sun was setting. There wasn't one bit of positive energy left in me at this point. I was miserable. "I am not a runner!" I shouted to myself!

The look on my face must have been obvious, because I remember some young college kid coming out to run a block or so with me. He was shouting words of encouragement over the roaring crowd that was now at my back, cheering me on by saying I was going to be an Ironman, keep going, etc. "Bug off, you young punk!" I wanted to scream. Go back to drinking your beer and let me drown in my misery. How *dare* you try to cheer me up. Don't you realize I have over 13 freaking miles left? But I politely nodded and murmured my appreciation. It was certainly sweet that he did this, but I was far too involved in my own self-pity party to take part in any joy taking place around me.

What was I doing? Who was I, to think I could do this? I was not an endurance athlete, and I was not a runner! Where was my family?

Many of the hundreds of people that I'd passed on the bike were now whizzing past me now, as I had slowed to a walk. I didn't care. I had lost all hope and enthusiasm.

That next six miles were a test for me, and I would discover the true core of what I was made of. Physically, I should have been done. It was only on my faith, stubbornness, and sheer will that I was keeping upright. Would this be enough? I really didn't know.

Bananas were no longer an option, as my body couldn't take it. I forced small sips of chicken broth down, as I knew I needed to keep up nourishment. The sugar and caffeine from the soda made it so I could get through to the next mile marker. This, too, was almost not enough. When your attitude sours, the body seems to follow.

My confidence, enthusiasm and excitement had completely disintegrated. There was not one ounce of positivity left in me. I was depleted — my tank was bone dry. I had turned into a ball of negative energy, and it grew more negative with each heavy and sloppy shuffle-step. I had prided myself on thanking each volunteer that had helped me that day; however, my thank you acknowledgements were reduced to a murmur as my head was now kept down. There were no smiles left in me. I quit saying my prayers of thanks to God. I was drowning in misery and self-pity as I shuffled my way to the next volunteer stop.

I missed my family more than ever.

At mile 16, I again saw my kids' sign. It was only God and my family that I could concentrate on as my body hurt with each small step forward. Keep moving forward.

I read the things they had written out loud. I vowed to myself that if I saw that sign among the myriad of signs on the way back, I would take it with me. That sign gave me a small glimmer of hope. I was still in a state of self-pity, but a little seed of hope is what I needed.

I thought about what the sign said. Maggie's saying of "Don't Quet" spoke to me again. Every so often I started remembering her words. "Don't Quet." "Don't Q.U.E.T." I kept trudging forward, but I was still in pain and felt miserable.

Darkness had now set in and the mile marker crowds had all but disappeared. There was a section, just before the turnaround, where the run took us through a park setting. This portion of the run had offered some solace and beautiful scenery during the first loop, but when I finally made it back for my second lap, there was nothing but darkness. The road was littered with unsuspecting potholes so attention to footing became a safety essential. It was lonely, as there were fewer runners out and we all were in no mood for chit-chat. There wasn't much sound, and the main light source was from the runner's primary accessory — glow sticks. We all just wanted to be done. By this time, most of us were wallowing in our silent misery. Our pain and exhaustion ever-evident by our grimacing faces and our lackluster pace.

I started to pray again and kept moving forward. If I stopped, I knew I wouldn't be able to keep going. It would be done. All that hard work and training for the past year would be wasted because I stopped. Keep going and "don't Quet."

Many athletes here had trained much longer and harder than me. I'd been a realist when I had carefully picked my training plan the year before, taking into consideration my additional commitments as an employee, a mom and a wife. I wanted to do an Ironman, but it needed to fit around our family life. Early in the training stages, my confidence wavered several times, when I realized that other athletes were already training heavily, while I was still in my early base-building phases. While they were out training heavy intervals, I followed my plan, even though I felt I wasn't training as hard. I knew I had to have faith in my plan, and stop comparing myself to others. This was *my* event and I was doing it for *me*. I just wanted to finish. I knew I wasn't there to take first place. First place to me meant finishing.

It was a surprise to see some of these hard training athletes, who were obviously in much better shape than I, shuffling along at the same pace I was. It was a slight comfort at the time, but not much. My legs felt like they were only moving inches at a time.

My feet never hurt so much in my life. My shoes felt like they were flat pieces of cardboard. I wanted to rip them away from my feet and toss them in the trash, never to be seen or worn again.

My shoes became an object of loathing and I convinced myself that I would never want them near me again. How could a person hate shoes so much? I will tell you how, when they feel like you are running on thin sheets of metal. I mentally was starting to snap. I was seriously beginning to "lose it."

I prayed some more and asked God for help. I needed Him.

Bright lights up ahead indicated the turnaround. Had I really made it to almost mile 20? Was I really only 6 ½ miles away from the finish line? I *only* had a quarter of a marathon left to go? Really?

My spirits started to lift little by little. My feet and body still hurt beyond belief, but I realized a glimmer of hope. Again, Maggie's words came to mind. Her "Don't Quet" saying was starting to repeat itself in my subconscious. As I neared the lights, I started to silently chant those words, "Don't Quet." And when no one was around, I spoke those same two words aloud, for my own benefit. Sometimes I would think in my mind "Don't" and spell "QUET" and other times I would say out loud "Don't Quet. Don't Q.U.E.T." It became my motto. Soon, I had a chant rhythm going in my mind, much like the story of The Little Engine That Could. "I think I can, I think I can." With each step that was taken forward, I repeated the words "Don't Quet."

I was starting to gain more hope now, and my excitement and momentum began to build. Then, it hit me as I rounded the cone that marked the halfway point on that second loop: I was going to be an *Ironman*! No longer was I wallowing in each step that I took. I was starting to look forward to the next six miles. Only 6 ½ miles stood between me and becoming an Ironman. I was going to do it. Nothing was going to stop me. I didn't care that I was exhausted, or that I hurt, or that it was pitch dark out.

It hurt whether I walked or ran, so I decided to start to "shuffle run." Each step felt like I was running barefoot on hot coals. I didn't care. I had trained for a full year for this. My family and I had sacrificed too much to stop. The amount of sheer discipline it took to get to this moment made me suddenly feel empowered.

During my training period, I had more "don't wanna do it" than "want to do it" days. When that alarm went off at 3:30 A.M., I awoke with dread more often than with enthusiasm. Once I started my workouts, I have to say I enjoyed many of them. There were no perfect weeks. Each work out session was taken one at a time. If a training session did not go well, I learned to leave it at the door. There were plenty of training sessions to be had and, if I let myself dwell on one bad one, it would only spiral into a ball of negativity that could potentially sabotage my plan and keep me from reaching my goal.

Each week contains 168 hours. How we choose to utilize these precious hours is up to us. My over-all 30-week training program consisted of six days of working out followed by one full day of rest. At first, it was hard not to feel guilty about taking a whole day off. I remained faithful to my plan and, although sometimes difficult, I didn't give in to temptation by doing a training session on my day off. After a few months, I learned that these rest days were just as important as my training days. My body needed time to recover. The bulk of my plan called for twice-a-day workouts. It averaged 12 hours a week over the 30 weeks, but in the final weeks it gradually increased to 20 hours per week.

My 168 hours a week went like this towards the end:

20 hours training

5 hours of travel, prep time (getting equipment ready, etc.) and wrap up time (showered, dressed, etc.)

40 hours at work

12 hours of commute time

49 hours of sleep (7 hours a night)

10 hours of movies with the family (No TV shows allowed)

2 hours for church

This left me with about 30 hours — if everything went as planned — to spend with my family, get our grocery shopping done, do some general house chores, etc. This sounds like a lot of time to spare, but really, it is not at all. It takes serious discipline to not whittle away these valuable hours on useless things that add no value to family, work, or training life. TV is a prime example of what I stayed away from. It's basically one of those mindless (non) activities that only serves to rob you of valuable time.

All that training and hard work was going to pay off. I was running my way to becoming an Ironman. By mile 20, I once again found MY sign among the hundreds of signs. It was a blessing from God. I picked up the 2x2 ft sign that my precious children had made, and vowed to carry it with me to the finish line. That sign represented the hope they gave to me. Their words of encouragement were a source of fuel and Maggie's "Don't Quet" writing became my motto. I chanted "Don't Quet," louder and louder, and over and over again. I was filled with hope, enthusiasm, and excitement. Carrying that sign made me feel like my family was right there with me, each step of the way. Even though they weren't there physically, I could *feel* them.

Those crappy shoes even started to feel better. It was as if God had put wings on them. To onlookers, it probably looked like I was barely crawling along, but inside, I felt like I was starting to fly. I was on my way to becoming an Ironman. All those days and moments of wondering if it was going to happen were coming to fruition, right here and right now! I was doing it!

I started to encourage others along the way, too. As I passed by some of those silent shufflers, I could see them crack a slight smile at seeing me moving forward with my sign. I was having fun, slapping people on the back as I slowly waddled my way past them. To some, I would say, "Don't quet — Q.U.E.T. because *you* are going to be an *Ironman*. We are both going to become *Ironman* athletes in just a few miles!" Most responded with a tired smile and/or a slight nod of acknowledgment. An acknowledgement that I knew was hard to do. It was very hard to talk, but I wanted to share some of my enthusiasm to others that looked depleted and hopeless.

Around mile 24, we could hear the blaring music and the roar of the crowd. "Can you hear that?" I would ask, if I came upon a fellow runner who looked especially dejected. "That is the sound of becoming an Ironman. Let's *go*. Some would begin walking a little faster in response. One guy looked *so* terribly sore. It almost hurt to watch him limp along. He could barely walk at all. "Let's go," I said, with gusto. He smiled a big tired smile, and started to limp along in a trot — as best he could — for a few steps. He laughed a little, and said, "You go on ahead." "Come *on*," I waved. "We are all going to make Ironman. Do you hear it? We're almost there." He tried to run a few times, but the effort was too draining. He assured me he would be fine, and encouraged me to keep going ahead. I turned, pointed to him, and yelled, with a smile: "*You* are going to be an Ironman." He waved me on ahead, with a big smile. It was fun to start to see the glimmer of hope and excitement come back into these human beings who were so physically spent. It was nice to stop focusing on the pain, and instead focus on the bigger goal of becoming an Ironman. To a spectator, it probably seems so easy. They can view the overall picture, and see the end. When you're a participant, however, it's hard to focus beyond those moments of extreme exhaustion and pain; the ultimate goal can easily become lost when the body is so emotionally, mentally and physically drained.

My body and feet hurt beyond belief by this time. Each and every single step brought a jolt of pain. I didn't care. I was grinning ear to ear at mile 24, and running as best as I could. I proudly clutched my sign as I moved onward. With every step, "Don't QUET" resounded over and over in my head. My smile got even broader as I got nearer to the finish line. I couldn't believe God was letting me do this!

When you come to the
end of your rope, tie a
knot and hang on.

—Franklin D. Roosevelt

CHAPTER 12

Ironman?

Now, there was only one more mile to go. One more mile! The crowd was *so* loud. I could hear the music clearly. One mile is *only* 12 more blocks. I am going to be an Ironman in 12 blocks! Thank you God for letting me have this moment. Thank you for making me physically able to accomplish this. Thank you, family and friends and everyone who trained with me!

A few blocks before the finish line, there was a huge crowd, several-people-deep, that stretched all the way to the finish line. I was running and *grinning*! Someone started to run alongside me. Low and behold, out of the thousands of people present, it was that sweet, enthusiastic young college kid whom I'd silently cursed earlier, when I was at my lowest moment. I was laughing and grinning as he ran with me, shouting words of encouragement. I thanked him.

I had wings. I was light as a feather. I could *see* the finish line. I could feel it, taste it and *see* it. What a beautiful site! My eyes welled up with tears of joy, and I held my sign above my head. People started to run to the finish line with me; they were cheering me on. I couldn't have had a bigger smile.

Only .30 miles left! As my feet pounded towards the finish line as fast as they could take me, I heard the most beautiful sound. The voices I heard are what I imagine the angels in heaven will sound like one day.

Those voices were the harmonious tones of my incredible, beautiful kids, along with my awesome husband and brother, shouting words of encouragement. Even with all of God's beauty around me, their shining smiles were the most heavenly sight I had seen all day. It meant the world to me, that they were waiting at the finish line. How fitting, that the family who had started this journey together would end it together.

I heard the announcer say, "Look, ladies and gentleman, she is carrying her own sign." I waved my sign as high as I could, laughing. As I neared the final steps of the finish line, I thanked God for my friends and family that had gotten me to this point. How very blessed I was.

Time went into slow motion for me as I savored each second as my feet were pounding the pavement as fast as I could run. I was just steps away from crossing the finish line. My goal, the one I had sacrificed for over the past year was only steps away now.

Then, *finally!* The words this large-boned, clumsy, non-athletic 38-year old person had waited to hear for over a year blared loudly, as my body broke past my finishers' tape. The booming voice was from Mike Reilly, the legendary Ironman announcer himself who had welcomed thousands across the finish line throughout the years — he said those sweet words that every Ironman triathlete dreams of hearing:

"Jen McDonough," (with the crowd screaming it with him) **"YOU are an IRONMANNNNNNNN NNNNNNNNNNNNNNNNNNNNNNNNNNN!"**

I had made it! Yesss! I couldn't believe it. Time stood still and I had to take it all in. Life is not a snapshot, it is movie. Even though my mind wasn't functioning at full capacity, and my body was starting to shut down, I was certain this moment, this particular snapshot in time would be burned in my memory for a long time.

I WAS AN IRONMAN!

A wonderful motherly volunteer put a wrap over my shoulders, and wrapped her arms firmly around my waist to guide me to get my medal and to have my finisher's picture taken. I could barely talk. Tears of joy were streaming down my face. I felt like I was going to collapse. I was beyond excited and beyond exhausted. I couldn't have grinned bigger when they took my picture. This was awesome!

The volunteer then led me to where my beautiful family awaited. She gently handed me off to them, where I was greeted with a barrage of hugs, kisses and smiles. I just looked at each one of their beautiful faces and silently thanked God. I could barely speak as I was overcome with emotions of joy.

A full year of wondering, each and every waking hour, if I could actually do this and I now sat with my family surrounding me trying to comprehend what I had just accomplished.

The journey that had begun over a year ago had now come to an end. My Ironman journey for that day had started at 7:00 A.M. with my toes hitting the water. It ended as my toes hit the finish line, some 14.42 hours later.

As my family talked excitedly around me, I was silent, so as to fully experience the joy of this moment, and to reflect on how thankful I was for having had this opportunity. We sat for a bit and I savored taking it all in with them.

After I ate a little bit (with my sweet kids picking off my plate) and after having completed a 140.6 mile journey minutes before (gotta love em), we went to watch the other finishers come in. I wanted a shower and a bed more than you can ever imagine at that moment. However, there was no way you could pry me from that finish line. As each finisher approached, I felt as though the crowd that I was now a part of, was virtually willing the runners to make it. They needed us. My body was covered with salt from the sweat of the day. To say my feet and body hurt was an understatement. I just wanted to lie down and sleep. Instead, we stood watching and cheering the remaining finishers on, with enthusiasm. As I write this, I'm reminded that each person who crossed that finish line also has their own unique story. With each new finisher, the crowd got louder and bigger.

Bob, who was extremely sick at the time, took the kids to bed around 10:30 P.M. We were due to leave for our drive to Disney in the morning and the crew needed their rest. As I watched him walk away, I marveled at how wonderful he had been. He had picked up the slack over the past year to let me train for this event. How grateful and appreciative I will always be for this gift. Sometime later we found out that he had pneumonia this whole time. I stood in wonder at his strength, kindness, and ability to encourage me, even when he was feeling at his lowest. He is truly a wonderful man, husband and dad. I admire him beyond measure.

Nothing is impossible, the word itself says "I'm possible!"

—Audrey Hepburn

CHAPTER 13

We Are An Ironman!

My brother and I stood fixated at that finish line, cheering louder and louder with each new person who crossed that marker. It was almost as if this congregation of strangers had bonded together in friendship as a result of a shared calling. I laughingly asked several exhausted athletes if they would do it again next year. The most common response? "NO WAY." A smile and stories of journeys had that day would follow. Problems that had seemed like major issues at the time, were now being expounded upon like showing off battle scars. Even my brother, who to this point didn't know much about triathlons, was caught up in the magic of the moment.

By 11:00 P.M., we were told that the roar of the crowd could be heard five miles away. As each person crossed, the crowd would yell their name with the announcer, while many of us raised our fists in the air, yelling: "You, are an IRON-MANNNNNNNNNNN!"

All around us, exhausted athletes crowded in. With each passing minute, our excitement for the runners, as they crossed the finish line was increasing. However, as the midnight cutoff time approached, our excitement was turning to anxiety for those who might not make it in time.

Those of us with medals around our necks knew the sacrifices each athlete had personally made to get to this point. It was heart-wrenching to think of others still out there on that dark course, who might not complete their Ironman journey.

It was 11:45 P.M. now, and the crowd was almost deafening. It was now that the announcer said that some runners had been spotted a mile or so away. "RUN!" you wanted to yell in their ears. "Do you know what time it is? You only have a little ways left." "You *can* do this," we silently willed!

Now the last 10 minutes neared, and the people coming in were barely shuffling across the line. Everyone was on their feet, willing these exhausted people to the finish line. "*Move!*," you wanted to yell!

While I admire the professional athletes for their discipline, sacrifice, and amazing physical abilities. I have even more admiration for the average everyday person — those who stepped out of their comfort zones, took a chance, and gave it their all — win or lose. These were people with real lives. Many worked full-time. Several had families. Some were stay-at-home moms or dads. Others were grandparents. Many had overcome incredible adversity to make it here. Each and every person had their own story. I was so thrilled to be among them, cheering on the last athletes as they came in.

These athletes coming in last were no different than those who'd finished earlier; We were *all* worthy of the "Ironman" title. It didn't matter if you came in first or last, we'd all completed the same course, with the same rules. We'd all pounded the same pavement and crossed the same finish line.

Now it was 11:56 p.m. The announcer called everyone's attention to the last runner in sight, the sole remaining competitor with the potential of finishing before midnight. The crowd became almost electric with anticipation in the hopes that this man would make it. His progress was *so* slow. Would he make it in time ? He shuffled along —*ever so slowly towards the finish line.* Many stomachs were clenched, as we willed him to finish.

As he inched forward, the crowd became strained with desire in the hopes that he would make it. I doubt he could hear a thing over the roar (I think they may have broken some sort of sound record). One last Ironman! I wonder what *his* story is.

At 11:58 p.m., our muscles strained with every step, as his feet reached their last step over the finish line. The crowd celebrated with one more deafening scream: "You are an IRONMANNNNNN!" Many were high-fiving each other, as if their favorite sports team had just scored. We felt as thrilled for this person as we were for ourselves.

The qualifying time was officially over when the clock struck midnight. Those who crossed the finish line after this time were disqualified. How painful it must have been for those who didn't make it, who'd still endured 17 grueling hours on the course. Many hearts went out to those who didn't finish. Some had decided to call it a night and be picked up, just miles from the finish line. I can't even fathom how they must have felt. *All that time and training, and they were so close!*

At about 12:02 A.M., the crowd started to roar with excitement, as it was announced that one more runner was about 3 minutes out. Even though he wouldn't be considered an official Ironman, I didn't see one person leave. At 12:05 A.M., a mere five minutes (300 seconds!) past the cutoff time, one more person crossed the finish line. The crowd went nuts! This man received the loudest cheers of the night, as well as a standing ovation. After being on the course for 17 hours, he had missed the cut-off time by only 300 seconds. That would equate to only about 12 seconds faster on each mile of the run-just a few more steps each hour. How heart-breaking!

Promptly after that person crossed, the bright lights and blaring music ceased. Just like that, it was over. The mob that had roared with an enthusiasm to match any Super Bowl game moments earlier was now reduced to hoarse whispers.

We were exhausted, sore, and smelly! We headed off to find our showers and beds. As I walked away, it was hard not to be sad for those were still making their way along the course — with no support, no waiting crowd, and no finisher's medal.

These people had outlasted the rest of us on the course, and were struggling to finish, even though it only meant they would simply finish, and be counted as disqualified. I said a silent prayer to give them strength to make it to the end of the course. These were the people with the most will, determination, and perseverance. When their toes hit that finish line, their achievement would equal my own, and many others... but it would happen in silence, with no fanfare

When I got back to our hotel room, I couldn't get those darn shoes off fast enough!, They seemed permanently attached to my feet as and I fought to get them off. As each one was extracted, I promptly flung it to the far corner of the room.

A hot shower had never felt so good. I relished in it. As the water poured over me, I was smiling. With my ears still ringing from the volume of the crowd, I thought, "Wow. I am an Ironman."

My brother Chuck and I stayed up very late, talking. Finally, around 2:00 A.M., I collapsed on the mattress, more physically exhausted than I'd ever been before. I was grinning from ear to ear. I had really done it. I was an Ironman. "Jen McDonough . . . You are an IRONMANNNNNN . . . " The phrase kept repeating in my head, over and over. It was a fitting lullaby for the night.

Always do what you
are afraid to do.

—Ralph Waldo Emerson

CHAPTER 14

Don't Quet!

My slumber was solid and sound that night. I woke up the next morning at 7:00 A.M., feeling physically tired, but on top of the world, emotionally. Had yesterday really happened? Was I truly an Ironman, or had I just dreamt I was?

I couldn't wait to finally do a little "shopping." I totally took in the sights and sounds of being with the same athletes I'd avoided days earlier, when I knew that doing so would be emotionally draining. Rather than the nervous anxiety that filled the air only days before, there was an atmosphere of sheer joy and camaraderie.

We packed up the van to drive to Disney.

As I was rushing out to the van to start our journey home, I looked over and saw a very tempting site. I couldn't believe it. There was an *empty* registration table, ready for people to sign up for next year's Ironman. It was minutes before registration would open online, and the spots would be filled up within minutes. I had heard over the past year how lucky I'd been to get into this event. It was one of the fastest filling Ironman events around. The empty registration table was right there, waiting for me. For a split second, I wanted to whip out my Visa card and say, "Bring it on." That lasted a short moment...then, I came to my senses, and ran to the van, without looking back.

When we piled in the van, Bob looked worse than he had all weekend. He didn't complain, he just looked like death warmed over — twice. It only took us about five minutes to make up our minds to skip Disney and get Bob back home to Minnesota. The kids were bummed, but they were good sports about it. As young as they were, they realized their dad was really sick.

Silently I sighed as my body had been through quite a bit of trauma just a few hours before. The thought of sitting in a cramped van for the 23 hour ride home didn't sound like fun, however, I knew we had to get my hubby home soon.

Before we left Florida, we stopped at a buffet-style restaurant. Other than being a little tired and having sore feet, I felt great. As we were enjoying being together as a family, it was easy to look around and spot my fellow Ironman athletes. Many of us were sunburned, walked with a limp, and looked tired. I SO wanted to stand up on a table, and yell, "*You are an Ironmannnnnn*" However, I didn't want us to get kicked out of the restaurant. Instead, I pointed, smiled, and loudly whispered "*You* are an *Ironman*," to several people we spotted on our way out. My family and I had giggling fits as we left. It was so much fun!

The drive home was pretty uneventful. Other than the first stop a few miles from the hotel, and a 20-minute fast food stop, we drove straight through to Minnesota. On the way, we spotted several Ironman painted vehicles. We would honk, and give an enthusiastic wave out the window as we drove by. It was a blast.

It was very late and dark outside when we stopped at a gas station in Illinois. Another minivan, similar to ours, was also filling up with gas. This Ironman-decorated van carried several kids, a dad, and an Ironman mom. Here we were, at this deserted gas station, in the middle of nowhere — two fellow Ironmen and their families. I quickly scanned around, and shouted across the gas station lot: "*You* are an *IRONMANNNNNN!*" pointing to her, with a smile. Her face instantly broke into a huge grin, and she started jumping up and down, as her family and ours exploded into fits of laughter. Their family yelled the same thing back to me. Even though both families were obviously tired, we loaded up on plenty of laughter for the remainder of our journey at that gas station.

A few days after we were home, I decided I wanted to have the memory of my journey tattooed on me for life. I worked with an artist, and together we came up with a design we liked. I had the tattoo placed smack dab above the back of my heel, where

I could easily see it, as a reminder. Each symbol was carefully chosen: The Ironman logo (a red dot for the letter "I," above the letter "M"), makes up the center. Below this are dark blue waves of water, to represent the scariest thing I had ever done — swim 2.4 miles, with sharks! Above the Ironman logo is a bike wheel, with my children's initials inscribed between the spokes. This represents my 112 mile bike ride, and the sacrifices my family made for me. On either side of the logo are my prized angel wings. They represent how God helped me, how he placed wings on my shoes to make me feel like I was flying at the end of the course, and also represents the prayers I said that day.

Beneath all of this are two words that still make me smile broadly, to this day: "Don't Quet." It is a permanent reminder of the wise words of advice from my young children: To just keep moving forward in life, no matter how much you want to quit.

When Maggie saw my new body art, she asked me how the word "quit" was spelled. She had a funny look in her 8-year-old eyes, when she asked me this. Not wanting her to think we were making fun of her, I cautiously said, "Well, most people spell it Q.U.I.T. However, the McDonough family spells it Q.U.E.T." It took a second, and then she understood. A big grin appeared on her beautiful face. "Mommmmm," she said. "Well," I said, "That is how WE spell it. Don't Quet. Remember that in life, kiddo. Just keep moving forward, and you will do well."

The sign that I had clutched so closely those last six miles of the course is hung in our garage, as I would like to get it framed someday. It holds a slew of memories, and is extremely precious to me. I grin at the memories it conjures up, whenever it catches my eye.

Looking back, was all the time, effort, and sacrifice worth it? *Yes*, it most definitely was! Not only did it have a profound effect on my life, but also my family. It reinforced some things that I had already known, and taught my kids that when you make extreme sacrifices to reach your goals in life, you will accomplish incredible things. Sometimes we have to skate on the edge of our self-imposed limits, in order to do extraordinary things, even when you think you are "not" whatever it involves.

Most of all, my journey taught me to be intentional with my time, to appreciate and use the gifts God has given all of us, and to push myself beyond what I think is possible. *If we put limitations on ourselves and only believe we can do the bare minimum to get by in life, then we will never experience our full potential.*

So, even though I was *not* a swimmer and *not* a runner, I sure am one heck of an Ironman. Believe in yourself, and trust in God. You will be amazed at what you can accomplish.

Live beyond awesome!

Thank you for reading our story. Please follow us on the rest of our journey by keeping an eye out for our *Living Beyond Rich* book due out in 2012. Our life would be turned upside down just two months after Ironman when we would receive life-altering news that one of our kids would be diagnosed with a lifetime medical condition. It would make us take a hard look at our lifestyle and how we would change how we lived and viewed life in order to accomplish a much bigger goal in life than Ironman. Here is where our real struggles in life would begin. . .

Please visit us at www.livebeyondawesome and/or follow me on Twitter at @TheJenMcDonough.

God bless and thanks for reading.

Jen

www.livingbeyondawesome.com

The McDonough Family 2011

Acknowledgements

To our friends and family, thank you for your suggestions, support, encouragement, and advice throughout this journey. We are very blessed to have you!

To the Ironman Staff & Organizers, your incredible events mean so much more than just another race. Ironman has helped shape me into who I am today and who I will be tomorrow. Thank you!

To Dan Miller and the 48Days.net gang, your wealth of wisdom, advice, suggestions, and excitement has made writing this book a blast. Thank you!

Weightwatchers, WW Crew, & Donna Beecroft, thank you for giving me the plan, support, and encouragement to take my weight off which allowed me to excel. Thank you!

Trish Englund, you are a marvelous content editor. Your humor makes the world smile. Thank you!

Molly Sanft, your talents go far and wide. You are amazing. Thank you!

Bill Conlan, you are an outstanding editor. Your generosity of time and gifts to me is staggering. Thank you!

To my "Bike Crew," I have enjoyed *almost* every mile with you. Thank you!

Jane, thank you for listening to my many woes since I was 8. I love you!

Chuck, thank you for being a friend, brother and the world's best uncle. I love you!

Moe, Lisa, Nicky, & Christian, thank you for being there for us. I love you!

Mom and Dad, your unconditional love, unbelievable support, and unwavering encouragement exceeds anything I deserve. Thank you for raising me to be a strong person. I love you!

Remy, I admire your persistence, your impish little ways, and your smile. You are going to be a fearless son of God and have a big heart just like your daddy, your big sister, and your two big brothers. I love you!

Max, I admire your big heart, your gift of empathy, and your ability to lead with your heart. You are a true son of God. You are going to lead so many people to Christ with your love for God and the joy in your heart. I love you!

Robbie, I admire your courage, your ability to teach, and your resilience. You are a true son of God. Just like your dad, you are going to be a great father when you grow up. I love you!

Maggie, I admire your gentleness, your gift of compassion, and your strength. You are a true daughter of God. I want to be like you when I grow up. I love you!

To my best friend and husband Bob, I have been blessed to be married to for almost 20 years. I admire and love you so very, very much. You are my rock. Thank you for believing in me and bringing out the best in all of us with your strong leadership, your wisdom, and your love. Who would have believed we would we be where are today? Living beyond awesome in this life and getting to be parents to the four best monkeys in the world. I love you.

God, thank you for every blessing and every lesson. I love you!

With ordinary talent and extraordinary persever-ance, almost anything is attainable . . . even for us *ordinary* people.

I wish I could do that, but. . .

What do you wish you could do?

Jen McDonough wasn't a swimmer, pro cyclist, runner, or even an athlete . . . but she was willing to see how far her God-given abilities could take her.

Unable to run two blocks, she decided to take on one of the most daunting physical sports around . . . Ironman Triathlon. This formidable race tests the limits of one's mental and physical endurance with a 2.4 mile swim, 112 mile bike ride, and 26.2 mile run all within a grueling 17 hour time limit.

The question: With three young kids, a spouse, and a full-time career, could she overcome her lack of natural athletic abilities and fears? Could she beat the challenges along the way and complete her journey?

In this heartwarming story of struggle and success, Jen explains why she, an ordinary, everyday mom and wife would attempt a seemingly out of reach goal like Ironman.

If you are facing an overwhelming challenge in your life, read *Living Beyond Awesome* and learn how you can beat the odds. Be inspired!

Connect with Jen through Twitter at @TheJenMc-Donough. Tune into her podcasts and/or join the LBA Challenge at www.livebeyondawesome. Be prepared to push yourself past your own limits.